Faith 101:
The Introduction to Faith

Atlanta, GA

ISBN: 9781944901271

Copyright © 2025 by Speaking Freedom LLC All rights reserved.

No portion of this book may be reproduced without written permission from the publisher or author, except as permitted by U.S. copyright law.

Book Cover by: Kaci Winslow

Publisher Website: speakingfreedom.org

Other Website Information: SpeakingfreedomTV.org, edu-freedom.org

Publisher Address: 75 Washington St. #1177, Fairburn, GA 30213

Speaking Freedom Book's Disclaimers

Welcome to Faith 101, The Introduction to Faith

We thank you for your purchase and look forward to helping you grow in all areas of your life.

We hope that you find all the information needed for your growth. God bless. Please listen to all disclaimers provided.

If you are currently under a physician's care, please maintain that relationship. This audiobook is not intended to stop your current treatment plan. If you need physician care, please seek out medical attention.

Please note that all results are based on the individual's ability to adapt and adjust to any given environment or situation. We are not responsible for your results. The life enhancement coaches at Speaking Freedom provide information to help you grow.

You are responsible for maintaining that growth, taking on and applying the information to your individual life as you deem needed and necessary. This book was written by Speaking Freedom Books concept by Kaci (Winslow) Myers.

For best results, you will need an open mind, the ability to research, and a balanced lifestyle.

Section 1: The Introduction

The goal of the introduction is to help you learn how to set your intentions.

In this book, we will be discussing faith. So during the course of reading this book, set your intentions on the things that you desire to learn about or get from this book. Meaning, get in your mind something that is a true heart's desire so that you can set your attention on understanding faith about obtaining that narrative, that mindset, that desire that you have deep down inside.

Please know that it does not have to be a person. It does not have to be a place or a thing. You may want to learn to have more faith in yourself and the things that you set out to do in your future. So I want you to focus on what you can apply the information to, based on the intentions of your heart and your goal set entering this course. And then on the other side of the course, we're going to also have you explain to us what you got from the course and how it varied or helped you understand how to move forward in your next stage, in your next level, in your next grace in living.

Throughout the course of this book, you will be asked questions. The questions are to help you think beyond your circumstances for the highest possible good. Here's your first question.

If you had one million dollars and you had no worries in the world, what would you do with it? Now, that question is full because I would like to know two things. What would you do with a million dollars? (If you're a millionaire listening to this, what would you do with a billion dollars? If you're a billionaire listening to this, what would you do with a trillion dollars?) How would you move differently? How would you seek to fulfill your sole purpose more? How would you make yourself more of a service to people? If you could do anything in the world, that you could imagine, what would it be? I want you to think about these things while you are learning about faith from Speaking Freedom. Throughout this book, think about your wildest dreams coming through and manifesting to truth for you.

I do want to give a disclaimer here because your dreams may not be the same as my dreams. Your dreams, your goals, and your purpose may not even be the same as your family members. So don't feel pressured or don't pressure yourself to try to live up to someone else's goals, someone else's ideal of purpose, someone else's ideal of living, or someone else's ideal of love.

This is the time when you define what all of these things mean to you. If you've listened to Spiritual Human Behavior, then you've already been working on yourself to understand your purpose better, to understand how to move beyond distractions, and to get to the next level of thinking and the next level of yourself. So now we're going to add how to live at optimum levels of faith.

And this is just the introduction to part one. If you would like to go back and listen to Spiritual Human Behavior, please go to the bookstore, or sign up to take the course.

The first question we are going to answer is: what is faith? If you ask any Bible-based religious person, they are normally going to tell you that faith is a substance of things hoped for and the evidence of things not seen, which is a biblical scripture that I like.

However, the actual definition of faith is complete trust or confidence in someone or something, a strong belief in God or the doctrines of a religion based on spiritual apprehension rather than proof, a system of religious beliefs, or a strongly held belief or theory.

Speaking Freedom develops theories, so of course, we support the narrative of faith; and how theories and doctrines can go together.

As a brand and a company, we do not push for religion. We push for the unity of all who believe in God, trusting that if you bring all parts together, you will get the "one unity" that we should have as believers of God, generally. So when you think of faith, what do you think when you think of faith? When I think of faith, I mostly think of trust, the belief in a system of God, mostly.

And I relate that to being able to have faith, have trust, have expectations for or about a certain set of circumstances, an outcome, or just the way my thinking will operate toward goals. Although in this particular book, we are not speaking specifically about religion, we will reference some things that people normally know as faith.

For more information about faith, please refer to our other book, The Unknown Power of a New Believer.

The Journal Thoughts are designed to be answered in the journaling space provided at the end of the book.

Section 2: Giving and Receiving

The first thing I want to do is identify what giving is. Giving is the outward gesture of love, care, and support.

It can be giving stuff, things, or time in general. The different forms of giving will depend on what you have available at the time of your desire to give. Again, giving can come in time.

What does that mean? Time means that you give people the opportunity to spend time with you. That spent time can be on the phone, in person, or on FaceTime. It could be via the time spent incorporating ideals together. Spending time is, for most people, the biggest element of love and how you identify those who love you because those who make time for you are those who love you.

People don't make time for things, people, or places that they don't love. So you have time. If you are thinking of what makes you feel loved as far as giving, you need to consider a couple of things.

Not only what makes you feel loved as far as giving and what you receive, but also what makes others feel loved as far as what they receive based on what you're able or willing to give. Everybody is not able to give what makes someone else feel loved or what others think they should receive. Giving has to be purposed by the person who desires to give. Then for giving to be effective, the person that you're trying to give in to must be receptive to the gift.

You can give into someone, you can give to someone, and you can give of someone. To give into someone is to say, here, I'm investing this into you as a person, as a being, as a soul, as a representative of the body of Christ along with me. You can give to a person here; I want you to have this. Or you can give of a person and to give of a person is to say, here, in dedication to, in honor of, I want to give this to you. Giving can also be considered a donation.

However, giving should be done without expectation.
Giving is one part of faith because it takes faith to give. It takes faith to allow yourself to open up to someone in either a vulnerable place, a tough place, or a place where you can allow yourself to care, and have concern for another person.

And on the receiving end, you can get gifts all you want to. But if you are not receptive to the heart behind the gift, if you're not receptive to what the actual gift is that you're receiving, then the reception of that gift will not be as strong. If you care dearly for something, your reception, your perception, the way you receive, and the way you look at the person who's giving will totally be different.

We talked about time. We talked about giving of, from, and to. And we need to talk about this part of faith, which is the giving of money.

Giving money is still giving, but not everybody is looking to be a charity case. So, giving money, stuff, or things will not always be sufficient as a gift to some people.

For myself, I am not a person that can be purchased. I don't feel appreciated just because you gave me a gift. A gift, a material possession, is not enough. I prefer, personally, to spend time with a person. That's the best gift because that's intimate. That's energy exchange.

That is more than just, here, here's a piece of paper, money. I spent time doing something so that I could take you the paper; versus giving you the time and coming together so we can get this paper together. So giving has to extend beyond finances because you can give your time if you are a person who believes in tithing and offering.

I am not trying to make you feel subject to disregarding your tithes or your offering. However, I don't want you to be limited in financial giving to a place when God calls more than just finances a tithe and an offering. To give of your time to God, to invest your gift to God, to offer more than enough to God beyond finances, will, in most cases, bring you more reward than just giving money.
Because you can give all your money and stay broke but not evolve or receive something on the other end. But when you give time, when you give energy, when you give hope, when you give gifts, you are establishing a place where you're opening up the universe, the divine center of God's energy, allowing you to receive differently because you're giving differently. And I want that to be something that people consider and think of because your obligation to fund a church cannot be mistaken as your obligation to give unto God what belongs to God and what belongs to God, not your money.

Your money doesn't belong to God. You can honor God with money, but in faith, your soul belongs to God. Your gifts were given to you freely from God.

Listen, you can use your gifts to make money if you so choose to do so. However, I don't want you to limit giving and receiving to money and finances. No funny money financing as the only means to give and to receive.

You have to be open to giving advice, too. You may have a word of encouragement and sometimes people need a word of encouragement even when they can't pay you for it. And a lot of times, especially currently in this day and age, there are a lot of people who want to be paid for the things that God showed them, grew them through, and allowed them to experience.
They want to be paid to help somebody else get through that experience, but God got them through for free. So I want you to see beyond finances when you think of giving and receiving. There are many other forms of giving other than money and finances or material possessions because at the end of the day when those material possessions are gone, will the love remain? Will the appreciation still hold value when those things become less valuable? So when you understand the different

forms of giving, giving of love, giving of time, giving of space sometimes.

Sometimes you need to give people space, it may not be a long-drawn-out thing, a breakup, or conflict. Sometimes people need to have the opportunity to gather their thoughts, to get themselves together, to get a better understanding so that they can proceed differently, more fully, more effectively. So I want you to understand the different forms of giving. Then I want you to focus your mind on giving towards your intentions.

What is your place of mind? Where is your heart when you're giving? Whether you're giving your time, you're giving your money, advice, your skills, your gift, your love, giving your support, or giving space allowing time to have its place and for grace, giving grace, mercy, or forgiveness in a way that you may not experience or a way that may be uncomfortable to you. Where is your mind? What is your purpose behind your gift? What are the intentions of your heart when you give? Because you have to have a heart to give. If you give because you feel obligated to give, then that's not really... I won't say it's not a good gift.

That's the kind of gift that is called a grudging gift. Like, oh, I hate to give it, but I'm going to give it because I feel obligated to. Don't give out of obligation.

Give out of liberty, out of freedom, out of vulnerability. If you're giving out of obligation, you won't give your best gift. You will give the bare minimum, do the least, and you will be unhappy with what you gave, how you gave, and whatever you receive out of it.

Now, it's also important to know not to give and do things solely for attention. Because if you give for attention, whatever good attention or bad attention you get, that's your reward. I mean, you might get something on the back end after the fact, but when you do things for attention, the attention that you receive is the gratification that you wanted for the validation that you think you need.

So it's good to know before you get to a place where you decide you want to give anything, have time to take it to God. Pray about it. Meditate on it.

Consult with God aka the universe about any gift given, and the gifts that you receive. Because you don't want to take gifts that's to hold you over, to buy you out, or to make you sway to one side or another because they gave you a gift. They think that it gives them favor.

So you don't want the gift to turn into a bribe on your end or the other end. The place that your heart is, and the place that your mind is at when you give, will change the way you perceive your gift. It will change the way that your gift is received.

Because if you give somebody something because you really want them to be happy because you've really observed everything, the situation, whether it's a place, a time, an encouragement. If you've done enough observation, meditation, and appreciation, then you're going to be able to give into the world & people from a different place. Because you're giving to them based on the observation that you've made that says, I know this excites, this moves, this causes a shift in the receiver.

And now you can say, I'm going to consciously shift the atmosphere. I'm going to consciously give time. I'm going to consciously feed into people's souls.

I'm going to consciously give advice. And when I do these things, I'm giving these things knowing that in my heart, it makes me feel like I'm doing something for God. It makes me feel worthy because I'm using my experience, my time, my money, my gift, my love, my effort to be a blessing to someone, to something, to some place in a very real type of way.

For most people, giving is healing. Giving in to someone can help you heal. To give advice to someone, you might speak something into someone else's life that also helps your own life.

So if you hold back a gift of encouraging word because you didn't get a payment, but God had a message for you, although you were supposed to give the message to somebody else, then you've missed your message because of a payment. If that experience was supposed to shift the culture and you didn't do it because somebody pissed you off, somebody did something that was unpleasurable, then you're in turn robbing yourself of the gift of giving. The gift of being a blessing is a gift full within itself.

Now, where's your mind at? Are you thinking this thing through? Have you made a conscious decision to give? Have you made a conscious decision to receive? Because receiving is allowing someone to give something to you, to accept something. And to receive and to accept something is just as important as giving. Because if somebody gives you a gift that they spent their hardearned money, they spent their time and observation learning, and they've done everything that they can, and then you don't appreciate their gift, it can change the way they perceive giving.

It can change the way they understand life. It can even change their vulnerability level and harden their hearts. You have to have the conversations that build the solid foundations for giving and receiving. Then build the exchange, that's built on a foundation of merit and love, even if it's I'm giving as unto God, so I'm giving this with a full heart, like I'm giving it to God, I'm going to give it to you.

I'm not charging God to give to him, so I'm not going to charge you to give to you. As is freely given, you give. Now, if you're paying for something, then that may not be a gift, because I'm not going to give you something that I'm still paying for.

That's regarding time, experience, in material possessions, that in any type of way you can slice it and dice it. I'm just not going to give away something that's not totally mine yet. I can't give you something that's not mine.

And when you get that in your mind, it can also change the perception of giving and receiving, because you give wholeheartedly, you're putting more thought into your gifts, you're putting more thoughts into what you're willing to receive, knowing that just because somebody gives you something doesn't mean you have to accept it. That may sound harsh, that may sound a little too bad, just for lack of better terms, you know, but you don't have to receive every gift that somebody gives you. If it's something that doesn't make you feel appreciated, if it's something that is not something that you really truly desire or want, then don't receive a gift just to take a gift, to say you got a gift. Taking something or manipulating a situation to have it for your advantage is still manipulation.

Taking something that you really don't want, just to appease someone is a form of manipulation, because you're not really happy, you're just pretending to be happy just to make them happy. The goal is full life joy, to enjoy life, not to be happy temporarily, but that giving becomes the cycle of your life that produces joy throughout the course of your life. Throughout your life, giving changes your mind, it changes your soul, and it makes you more receptive to learning and growing.

Listen, I don't want you to limit God through limiting your giving. If you're only giving God what you feel comfortable with, then you're limiting God. If you're only giving God finances, then you're limiting God.

God wants to use you, your soul, through your vessel, which is your body. God wants to be able to use you here on earth. If you believe that you're an earth angel, if you believe that you have more to give and a lot of love to give, then allow God to use you unlimited.

Don't say, well, God can use me here, but he won't use me over there. In order to be effective, you have to be versatile. You have to be willing to give outside of your comfort.

You have to be willing to receive sometimes outside of your comfort. Now, that does not mean to sell your soul or to not pursue your purpose under the context that you're giving outside of your comfort or you're receiving outside of your comfort, but don't limit God. If God wanted to do a new thing with you, if the universe wanted to start something new through you and God/the universe suggests that you give certain things to make way for the things that he has to give to you so that you can open doors for somebody, that will open doors for somebody, that will in turn full circle open a door for you in a way that you may not think about when you're giving the gift! When you're being encouraging, when you're helping people grow, when you're giving finances, even to a church, hopefully, you're giving to a church that gives back into the community so that if by chance you ever need a bereavement gift or you ever have a struggle and you need some financial help from the church, they are willing to and able to give back into you.

Honestly, we're not looking for who has the most or who's done the most, we're looking for the most authentic faith. And I say we're looking for because as you begin to develop and grow your level of faith, your level of giving, the mindset you have surrounding giving and faith, you'll begin to request more, want more, desire more because you will know that you deserve more, but you have to take the limits off of God. You have to allow God the opportunity to show you what he has for you.

You have to be willing to give into what's presented and present for you. Now everybody's limits or limitless may be different. Don't try to base your life on the living, giving, or receiving scale of the next person because that person may have a different life path than you. If you're giving based on somebody else's life path and not your own life path, then you may give into the wrong things and expect things that you can't get because that's not meant and can distract you from where you're supposed to be.

So the goal has to be from your soul to say, okay, dear universe, dear God, what do you have for me? Show me the process of faith within giving that will help me to accomplish, to reach, and to accept the plan and the purpose of life that you have for me. Remove all limits from my thinking, from my being, from my understanding, and allow me to see the fullness and greatness of you, God, the universe, the divine energy that connects, resonates, and makes my body alive through my soul. So what does limiting God mean? To limit God means to say, you know what God, you could do this but I don't know about that.

To limit God is to say, well, I'm going to put a cap on what
I'm willing to do which means I am putting a cap on what I'm willing to receive. Sometimes willingness

outweighs having to do. Sometimes God wants to see if you're willing.

Are you willing to make the sacrifice? You may not have to make the sacrifice. You may not have to give this. You may not have to do that.

But are you willing to go the extra step? Because limiting God is saying, I hear what you want, God, but I'm not willing to go that far. I'm not willing to believe that much. I'm not willing to sow or encourage or perceive or be bigger.

Sometimes you limit God by limiting your evolution. And we want to ensure that when we're walking in faith when we are practicing faith, when we're getting to know the basics of faith, that we remove all limits from ourselves, remove the limits of religion, remove the limits of what your mama told you you needed to be, what your uncle said, what your grandparents said. You have to share everything to allow God to restore your faith that will take you to what you're meant to see, to whom you're meant to be, to the places you're meant to go, and to the things that you are meant to do.

But you cannot expect the fullness of God while limiting, even limiting God to a Bible, limiting God to only the church, limiting God to only this place or to only that person. Take the limits off of God. Be able to see God in giving and receiving all around the world and all around you.

Take the limits off of your mindset regarding what's a gift to God or unto God. What are you willing to do to see your highest faith activated? What are you willing to give to help the world shift into a better place? What are you willing to give God? Who are you willing to grow to become? If God told you right now, stop what you're doing, I need you to make some adjustments, and I need you to do this instead of doing that because this will be more prosperous long term. Would you be willing to become more than you imagine yourself to be? Are you willing to see God in a way that you could have never imagined yourself seeing God work in your life? Can you imagine the favor of God being on your life because you've opened up your heart, your soul, your mind, and your life to the fullness of God?

The next question is, what can you let go of? What are you giving yourself into that you can let go of? What time restraints can you let go of? What places and people can you let go of? Because you're giving your time into places, you're giving your life into things, and the things that you give yourself into effect everything around you and about you.

So you have to know what are you willing to let go of. What are you willing to do differently? Who are you willing to become with your gift, with your mind, with your work, with your life? What will make you different? How will you stand out? What makes you... you? Just in regards to giving, what makes you a different giver than the next person? What makes you more faithful than the next person? Not the number of times that you do it, but the intentions of your heart and the depth of your mind when you're giving, when you're extending your hand to offer a resource, to offer encouragement, to offer time, to offer a gift. You have to be sure that you, one: are confident, and two: that you are willing and free about giving. And then you have to be open and honest with yourself.

Again, giving is way beyond tithes of money. To tithe means to give of your time as well as your money. If you don't have money, but you have time, do you stop tithing because you don't have money? No, you find a way to give of your time, to give of yourself into the things, into the people, into the situations, into the circumstances that you would like to see for yourself.

Confidently. Giving beyond money will move your soul in a way that you've never known. The reality is that money only has as much value as we give it.

And your time is invaluable because you can never get it back. You can spend time to get more money. You cannot spend money to get more time outside of surgery. When I say surgery, if you have a short life to live or the doctor diagnosed you with something and you can have surgery that can heal you and make you better, that's the only way you're going to be able to use the money to buy more time.

Aside from that, you're only renting time or allowing people to rent your time. So what are ways that you can expand your giving? Currently, if you're a tither of money to a church, how much more and what other type of tithing can you offer to others? Can you tithe a percentage of your time into giving of yourself? Can you tithe a percentage of your business? Can you tithe peace? Can you sacrifice enough to give more of yourself, to give more of your time, to give more of your knowledge, more of your information? Expand your mind by expanding your thoughts towards the things that you desire to receive and that will help you expand your mind to the things that you desire to give. The last thing that I would like to say on this particular topic about giving and receiving is to ensure and make sure that you do not forget to give into yourself, to feed into yourself. Before you begin to feed all these things that you desire to give to others, make sure you are replenished, make sure that you are sufficient, make sure that you are in a position where you know what you want because you've given it to yourself and now you can give it to others as unto yourself.

Section 3: Prayer

Prayer is something that most people are familiar with by term, but the goal here is to help you understand what prayer is, and the intimacy that it contains, and make sure that you understand how to use prayer to the best of your ability to push and comfort your faith. So first, you should know that prayer does not have to be some super deep formal conversation that you're having with God where you can't simply be yourself.

A prayer is not a religious process as much as it's a deep intimate conversation that you have with God. You have two different ways that you can pray, of course. You have the prayer that you say within yourself and then you have the prayer that you speak out loud.

Now, if you're really advanced or really spiritual, then there is also the prayer of tongues and the language that you may not understand that may be ancestral or a divine revelation. Through praying in tongues God's spirit speaks to himself in a language that God within you can understand. I know that that was a bit much or at least it seems that way on the surface level, but prayer is like talking to yourself, and encouraging yourself because in order to believe in God, you have to first believe in yourself. You have to first speak to yourself the way that God would speak to you or else when God speaks to you, you will tune God out thinking all types of things.

Prayer is beyond religion. It is beyond a formal way of asking God for things. Prayer should be a conversation.

Prayer should be an intimate detail, thought, projection, and sometimes the reception of information that you can receive during what's kind of like a meditation. Of course, you can be formal. You can say, dear God, make your prayer request and amen.

You can pray the prayer that's in the Bible. "Hallowed be thy name, thy kingdom come, thy will be done." You could do all of those formal things, but God, the universe of this divine energy that has us here, desires intimacy.

That is a conversation like you would talk to your mother, a conversation like you were talking to your best friend. The conversation that you have with yourself when nobody else is around, whether you're encouraging or discouraging yourself is a form of prayer and meditation. Now, depending on what it is that you're focusing on could tell me if you're praying or you're worrying.

And to worry is to focus on all of the negative, or the worst things that could happen. Okay, I need to foolish proof this because there is a difference between not focusing on the negative, being negative, and considering all things. Whenever you are praying, meditating, or if you are bringing something to pass that you're trying to manifest, you do need to weigh all possibilities.

If you are setting your intentions for something specific, it is always good to learn how to focus your attention and your energy on the positive things. Now, you always need to make sure that you consider all things. That means considering all the positive possibilities, but also considering all of the things that could not go your way; So that you are progressing by evaluating the possibilities, the things that could go wrong, and the things that you desire to go right.

Then you can make your adjustments based on those things. Because if you don't consider what might go wrong, then how would you be able to proactively make sure that you're prepared to be successful? If you consider all things, if you count the cost, saying: to be successful, in order to set this manifestation towards me, I have to both consider the good, the bad, the highs, the lows, then I have to adjust as I move towards that first, in my mind before it begins to be in my movement.

So you have to make sure that you're focusing on the positive and not only on the negative because that is considered worrying. But when you focus on the positive and you speak into existence, the positive things and ask for guidance and tell the universe, expressing to God how you truly feel as if nobody else is in the room as if nobody else can hear you, that it's just you and God. And God is saying, you know what? Talk to me the way that you would if you were confident that I was your friend if you were confident that I was going to protect you.

If you were confident that I loved you, how would you speak to me? Don't consider what other people would consider respect. If you feel pissed off, then say, you know what God? Right now I'm frustrated. I'm pissed off; Help me.

Prayer should not only be about getting help. You may pray and say, you know what? I want to do better.

Make me better. And there's a difference between saying, I want to be better to help other people; versus those that say, I would like to receive stuff and things so that I can look better. Being better means that you're going to evolve and adjust to the world around you. Looking better is just saying, I want to be flashier. The goal of prayer and faith mixed together is to grow your soul as you grow what you hold on the outside.

Prayer is not religion or religious.

It is a conversation that you're having with the closest person to you where you can express yourself as freely as possible and trust the guidance and the response from the universe/ God that you're going to get back. Now, let me just tell you, if you don't pray the way that you would speak your true feelings, then you get frustrated and you start complaining. Let's say you're in the car talking to yourself and you're talking about, oh, this is how I really feel and you are not expressing that to God, God still hears you. God still sees, understands, and processes your frustration.

It's just that you're not being directly forward with God about how you feel so that God can give you peace so that God can assist you in ways that you wouldn't be able to comprehend if you had not come directly to God. To pray effectively, you must be honest with yourself to hear from God. You must be honest with God.

Again, this is the one-on-one conversation that you're having with your best friend and the entire universe. There is nothing that you can do that make God turn away from you, but you could turn away from God. There is nothing that you could do that God would make you suffer in such a way that he wouldn't be there to comfort you in that suffering, but you could turn away and suffer on your own if you're not sticking closely to God's plan instead of just going on your own.

The goal is to understand that, to be honest with yourself, to love yourself, to embrace yourself, to get a full understanding of who you are at whatever point you are in life, because if you can be honest with yourself, then you can be honest with God. If you can give God your all, then God will replenish all of that within you and in this world forever. So to be honest with God is to be honest with yourself because if you're in denial like people who use Christianity and the Bible to act like they don't have a past, which is really unhealthy. When you begin to embrace every single part of your struggle, every single part of your past, every single experience, then you can say, you know what God, this is who I am, I understand who I am, I accept who I am and I'm asking you to use me as I am.

I'm asking you to show me as I am, to heal me as I am, to protect me as I am and what does that mean as I am? That doesn't mean that if you see or have or notice some ways about yourself that are unpleasant you just say, oh, this is who I am. No, it means that you're working, growing, and overcoming, despite any shortcomings, despite any harm, abuse, disregard, or neglect that you felt in your life. If you felt abandoned, then prayer is the time when you say, I did feel like this, and not only did I feel like this, God, I need you to help me not to only get over this but to restore this and to do that. Then in that honest conversation that you have with God is an honest conversation that you can have with yourself that allows you to go further and beyond, that allows you to heal and help others heal because you are willing to accept who you are. When you are willing to accept your struggles and you are willing to see how that evolved you into who you are, you can ask God through prayer and meditation how to use you to the highest levels of your ability and there is absolutely no wrong way to pray.

I don't care if you cuss, I don't care if you fuss, I don't care if you cry but the goal is to have intimate communication and fellowship with the universe/ God on this earth and then allow the universe/ God to manifest your answers back. When I say manifest your answers back, I know you're probably thinking like, well how does the universe/ God manifest answers back? The universe/ God has quite an interesting way of interacting with us through radio, TV, animals that we see, experiences that we have, random conversations, interactions, synchronicities and so many other things that we have to realize that God is speaking to us when God is speaking. There is no wrong way to pray, there is no wrong communication with God, and there is nothing that you can do to say: oh God is going to be upset, God already knows your past, present, and future, everything about you he accepts because he created you to get through the mess.

When you realize that, then you will speak to God in prayer as your closest friend and ally. It is very important that you pray for what's really important to you. Don't make generic prayers, don't pray for the things that you think that God would be pleased with based on your praying.

Pray for what really matters to you, pray for the things that you're passionate about, pray for the things that affect your heart and your soul because those are the things that you are called and drawn to pray for. Those may be some things that you are called and drawn into being a part but you have to make sure that while including yourself you also pray for what's important to those around you. Pray to understand yourself better, pray to understand your spouse better, pray to understand your children better.

The goal is to just make the communication so clear and direct with God that we have no doubt, we have no shame, we have no emptiness within our brain. While talking about prayer, I do want to say this, I want you to know that going to church is great, the fellowship with other people is great. However, your body is your temple, and church attendance alone doesn't guarantee God's attention.

Just because you pray in church does not mean that God hears you more than when you pray at home.

God desires a personal relationship in which communication is key. If you've ever been married or in a serious relationship then you know how key communication is.

God's connection within you, possesses a likeness to God. So, you need to align yourself with knowing who you are in God, and through God. Know that God created you to be able to survive the things that you were created and destined to survive. Then that means that he accepts you and likes you because you are made in a portion of his image.

You are made like the universe, the likeness that God finds as a connection with us will help you to understand and grow deeper in your prayer life and connection with God. Because you are made in God's likeness, he accepts you. He wants to communicate with you... Please know that I say, "he" for lack of better terms, the universe/ God desires constant communication so that you can know yourself so that you can be attuned and aligned with the purpose for which your soul was created on this earth for.

Journal Thoughts

How can you begin to pray more efficiently or effectively?

That means taking time to talk to God on a day-to-day basis. How can you talk to God more?

How can you make that a communication that's more effective than any human communication?

Now praying over meals is one thing, praying before bed is another but making a constant commitment of continuous communication with the universe/ God can save you so much time, and so much money and help you keep your energy recharged every day so that you can reach the goals and the things that your heart desires. I would like to add that I don't want you to think that you have to be in church to learn how to pray, to pray, or to talk to God, period.

I want to make sure that you understand that your connection with God is your connection with God regardless of what anyone says, regardless of how anyone tries to make you feel, or regardless of any outside connection. You are connected to God because you are a living, breathing human who knows how to understand the concept of the universe aka God.

Section 4: Hearing From God

Following the section about prayer, I want to reintroduce or introduce to you how to properly hear from God, how to understand hearing from God, and how to turn on your listening ear for how and when God speaks. "How God Speaks" is explained further in the book Spiritual Human Behavior, as well as learning how self-awareness helps you understand how God speaks to you.

To hear from God, especially when you're setting your intentions or believing for something by exercising your faith, you have to be open to God's plan.

Honestly, I know that sounds very cliche but you have to really be open to the possibilities that God could put in place. In previous sections, I talked about knowing how God may align things or how God may open doors, how God talks, and how to listen. So right now it's about allowing our minds to consider all the possibilities.

Weigh the good and the bad to know the potential for success, while considering the bad things that may take place that could delay the success of the goal. When you begin to calculate the cost of whatever it is that you have your intention set on or your goals, you begin to open yourself up to God because you're already calculating what could go right or what could go wrong. Then you have to give room for God to make use of the universe and God's favor to allow things to come into your life.

Being open to God is knowing the possibilities and then being open to "the more" that could go right. It's not limiting God. It's not saying, okay, well, I can only believe that you can do so much.

It's taking on the thought, I've prayed about this and I believe that God can do this. Now let's see how big God will make it. So ensure that we don't want to bottle off ourselves thinking that the thing that we want to do will overpower what God has planned.

If we do overpower God's plan by doing our own thing, then there will be some favor that may be missed because we're doing something out of God's plan. Your question might be, what is God's plan? Well, it's a part of your vision and your dream for yourself. What are the things within yourself that you can't let go of or relax about? Is there a dream life or goal that you constantly are reminded of regularly? When you work towards it, does it set your soul ablaze in a way that even your anxiety goes away? In some cases, the tasks may seem overwhelming until it is started and then it flows with ease.

When you begin to open up your mind to God's plan, then you will have to also be open to the suggestions that God may present. Because if God tells you something that you're not open to, then you won't believe it's God speaking to you. And that's a hurtful truth.

So, I want you to do a couple of things during your time of praying. I want you to ask God for specific signs that you could believe. Signs that things will align so that when you see it, you know that that's the sign that you requested. Seeing a sign could make you feel confident in the favor that you're speaking. When you begin to pray, you have to say things like, okay, God, if you desire this for me, then show me the best way to make it happen.

Say, show me a sign, and be very specific about the signs that you desire to see. Understand that God can send you a sign, but if you're not open to receiving the sign, then the sign won't seem like it was sent because it's not open to be received. So you have to ask for signs and wonders, ask for God to speak to you, and send a message to you in ways that are not ordinary.

The way God works and the way God speaks, God may send somebody to you that you've never known before, to warn you. God may give you a dream that displays certain things to make you aware of something that you may have to face or see. You have to be able to find ways to communicate with people while allowing God to communicate with you through other people.

Here are the ways that God communicates: God communicates through people you know, random messages, strangers, and simply the world around you. If you ask God for a sign and then you see a butterfly, that could be a sign for you.

If you ask God for a sign, then if someone comes to you and says, you know, I heard this or I felt this in my spirit and I needed to let you know. And it's impactful, something that nobody could know unless they were speaking to God or God was speaking to them on your behalf. That's a sign.

That's a wonder. Sometimes the phone can ring and it may be a plan of God that you don't quite understand just yet. But you again have to be open to the fullness of God's plan despite what you may be thinking.

There are always "holdups, paradoxes, and other things" that you can find in Spiritual Human Behavior theories that can help you identify distractions. But your focus is on setting your intentions, what you're believing God to manifest with & through your faith for you as well as to you. And then being open to allow God to speak.

For example, you may get something in the mail. You may have prayed about something and ask God for a sign and then tomorrow you get a check in the mail. Honestly, it may not be tomorrow. It may be a week from now, but you have to be ready, be willing, be open, and be consistent with what you prayed and asked God for. Then believe that it will turn up in a way that you can receive it and understand that it's God sending his blessings to you. God really sounds simply like peace. Sometimes you may feel anxiety that God gives you peace about. You may feel uncertainty, but God gives you peace about it.

When you're going to hear from God, when you're wondering what God sounds like and how to give God your listening ear, you really have to consider the peace that comes upon you whenever you're facing a difficult issue. Consider how you feel after praying when faced with a dilemma or anything that challenges you to grow, to become better, to become whole, or to evolve into the best version of yourself. Because I'm telling you now, when you begin to exercise your faith, faith is not always the safest option.

Faith would normally give you some type of anxiety because it's something that you have to trust God to accomplish. So when you begin to exercise your faith, know that there will be challenges that will come to present a struggle. Whether you struggle or not will depend on how prepared you are to face difficulties that may come on the path that you were designed to take.

This is the reason why we "consider all things" when planning because you may be going down a path. And if you've never thought of the challenges that you could face down this path, then you may consider it a struggle. But if you consider the things that could come about while you're on this path, then it may be a challenge, but it won't be a struggle.

The difference between a struggle and a challenge is that a challenge is something that you can overcome that is difficult but workable, fixable, and doable. It may put a little bit of pressure on you, but it's not going to defeat you. While a struggle is something a little bit more difficult than a challenge.

Struggles might take a little bit more out of you. It might make you feel a little bit more depressed a little bit more down or a little bit more frustrated, especially if you're not prepared to face the things that are ahead of you.

Being prepared could sometimes come from communication. It definitely comes from prayer, meditation, and having that time alone so you can figure out what you're going to do, and figure out how to execute the plans that God is showing you. This may be through a vision board, through a dream, through a vision, or a waking vision that you are able to visualize. You have to be able to put things together so that you can exercise that faith. While you're exercising that faith, when it seems like a struggle and it's just a challenge, you will be able to overcome it.

You won't have to be stuck, at any time because you already pre-planned for some things that might happen. And that creates a lighter load for you. It removes the barriers so that when things come, you don't feel overwhelmed.

You're thinking should be, "so I figured something might happen because this is a new path. This is a new journey. I am learning.

I am growing. For me to continue to grow, the old things that used to be hard will become easy, and new challenges will come. But I won't struggle because I am way beyond the temptation to struggle by the way that I pre-plan and prepare for success down this path."

Earlier we mentioned meditation because it is very important that you take some time not to ask God for anything, not to make any type of request, but to give God time to speak to you, to give you ideas, to give you new things on your mind so that you can develop and grow with. How do you meditate? Meditation is just having some quiet time. In meditation, you may do it in various ways.

Quiet time can mean a lot of different things to a lot of different people. For a mother, a couple, or a father who has children who are full-time parents, then quiet time might be a glass of wine. It could be some slight jazz music where you can just sit around, think about, consider, and allow God to pour into your soul. God will show your spirit the things that you should know, the things that you should adhere to, and the things that you need to adjust so that you can have better follow-through.

Meditation is not spooky; it's the time of listening. It's the time of really taking time to say, "Okay, I've made my requests unto God, to the universe, and now I'm going to make way, clear my head, clear my space, so that the universe can converse with me." When you're meditating, you may hear an idea.

You may see something or feel something in your heart that you need to jot down. You may see a picture in your mind that you need to draw or make note of what you're seeing so that later on you can reference the same thing if it becomes a Deja vu or something like a dream. The goal is manifestation when we are exercising faith because we're not using faith to do life.

I'm not exercising my faith by just using my faith to make sure that I'm living and I'm breathing. However, faith is the substance of things hoped for and the evidence of things not seen. Faith is the extra mile, the thing that you aren't sure of but you know if you make this one move or you do a thing or two then something new can be produced.

So you have to be able to meditate sometimes with "that thing" on your mind. Sometimes meditation can be a long drive in silence. Sometimes it might be the radio on.

Again, it may be a glass of wine where you are able to sit down, unwind, and take a load off. In order to meditate, you have to be able to clear your mind. In order to hear from God, you have to be able to hear from God clearly by clearing your mind of the clutter.

So it is very, very, very important for you to be able to find a time, whether it's 10 minutes, or 20 minutes to say "Father, I thank you for this peace of mind. I thank you for giving me peace in uncertain situations and I allow you to be one with me and to communicate with me I am open to you, I sit in silence, and I wait for you to commune with me to continue moving forward with the ultimate peace." And you sit there with your notepad.

You can write down thoughts, plans, and ideals. You may meditate while creating a vision board. A vision board is a collage type of effort where you put together the things that you would like to see in your future or want to be forever. Just to be clear, meditation is big in faith because you have to get direction. Your direction comes from praying, giving, and receiving and that could be giving prayers, receiving an invitation of Christ's likeness, opening up your heart to more fulfillment, to be fulfilled, to have your faith exercised, or for your faith to be fulfilled and for you to be able to manifest the intentions of your heart.

You do need to honor giving and receiving regardless if it's financial or not. You do need to have time where you speak to God about your deepest heart's desires and then you need to have time where you make time to hear back from God. Now with the universal energy of love and oneness, you have to open your heart to love and true oneness because we are the universe and the universe is literally who we are.

You have to find a quiet place where you won't be bothered for at least 10 to 20, maybe 30 minutes. Give God the opportunity to speak. Turn the radio off sometimes.

Turn your TV off sometimes. Sit and be quiet with yourself. I know it's a little daunting to be alone or to sit with your thoughts but if you're always running from your thoughts then you'll always be running from yourself. Instead, learn to not allow certain thoughts to take root so you can address what you are thinking and then sort it out in a way to determine whether you're going to continue to think about it, whether you're not going to think about it or what you need to do to move forward in the most progressive way possible.

Journal Thoughts

Considering meditation, for the last thing in this particular section, I want you to think of a place where you can meditate. Think of a way that you can work for at least 10, 15, maybe even 20 minutes a day. Now if you're good, and you can work in an hour of meditation, whether it's 30 minutes here, 30 minutes there, or 20 minutes spread out to equal up to the entire 60 minutes, you will begin to see the light and feel lighter as you begin to move forward in manifesting your intentions.

So right now, identify the places that you feel comfortable in meditation so that you can begin to see yourself meditating and receiving all the answers that you need to move forward in meditation.

Section 5: Sacrifice

Let's talk about sacrificing because a lot of people think that sacrificing means going without something, losing something, or something being taken away/ forbidden. And the reality is that sacrifice in alignment just means that you don't do the things that you used to do.

For me, as I grow and in order to grow, it may take me sacrificing going out some. It may take me changing something so that I am able to focus on better things. So to make time to pray more, in order to make time to meditate more, to hear from God or to exercise your faith in other areas, you may need to make some adjustments to your day-to-day life.

Initially, it can seem hard. It might seem like you're losing out. But when you begin to see the progression of alignment, then sacrifice is just saying, you know what, I'm doing what's best for me, versus how I used to do what was best for others.

Does sacrifice mean losing something? No, sacrifice means being different. Sacrifice means being willing to stand out, to be talked about, to be looked upon funny, and maybe even judged sometimes. Because sacrifice means that you're willing to make some changes to your life and adjustments that will make you better.

Some things, again, may not be things that you're comfortable with or what you like currently. When I say that you may not like being alone initially, dealing with your own thoughts, your own emotions, or not having anybody around to tell you how you should feel; that means it may be uncomfortable at times.

Faith isn't always doing what's safe. Sometimes taking the risk of doing something different, doing something purposeful, seems like a sacrifice because of the ridicule that you may face or because of the objection or rejection that you may deal with. So it's not about losing something, sacrifice is really about gaining. You will realize this as you begin to align with and learn your purpose, as you begin to accept yourself and embrace yourself for all that you truly are below the surface. After a while, you will begin to say, you know what? Maybe those people are not healthy for me. Maybe that situation is not perfect or right for me, although it may be good for someone else close to me.

Be willing to be different. When are you willing to say, "You know what? I have to admit it. I'm going to have to sacrifice trying to look cool on this occasion with these people because this is my truth and I'm willing to stand in my truth."

Purpose will definitely cause you to travel a path that everyone is not capable of traveling. The things that you may be good at with or grace to do, may cause someone else to fall to the wayside. When we hear people in general say that everybody can't go, it means you have to sometimes cut the fat.

Sometimes you have to remove the people who aren't really supplementing your growth to help you on this journey. Some people sometimes are around to slow you down. Now they may not be doing it intentionally, but if they're not feeding into your purpose, helping you grow, and accepting who you are as a person so that you can become the person that you're called to be, then that might be a relationship that has to be sacrificed.

And to be completely honest, if it's not a healthy or a truly good relationship, then you're really not losing if you're bettering yourself. So sacrifice can come on this path because you have to begin to align with the things that you need to be aligned with. So if you've already tried too much, at any time you can say, "Hey, I've gone so far, but you know what? I think I need to get with God and ask God how to take me to where I desire to be. I need to pray and meditate within the universe and ask the universe to guide me."

If you do that, don't be surprised when you begin to go down a path where you're losing people who are not really for you or you're losing jobs that are not really for you. Remember your prayer and that you are losing the things that kept you bound and feeling desperate, things that were void fillers instead of purpose fulfillers, then you will begin to learn what it means to sacrifice. You may sell a home, but you may get another one on the other end.

You may have to experience divorce so that you can be happy and purposeful, but that does not mean that you won't get married on the other end. Sometimes sacrifice seems like a loss until you are able to see the lesson in the things that you are enduring and the things that you are experiencing.

There are different forms of sacrifice.

Saving money can be a sacrifice. Not buying the things that everybody else is buying could be a sacrifice, not partying like everyone else is partying so that you can focus on your goals, build your empire, and spend time with your family may feel like a sacrifice. Having focus will seem like a sacrifice to those who are constantly distracted, to those who are constantly trying to find the next best thing, those who are living in the future or have become destination addicts where they're always seeking to go to the next place. Focus or having tunnel vision on your specific goals could help you go even further distance in relation to faith.

Parenting can be a sacrifice for some people because some people are willing to give up their entire lives to make sure that they're a good parent; while you have others that will sacrifice being a parent so that they can still enjoy their lives. It's just a matter of what is a priority for you in your life at this point. What are you trying to manifest? What do you want to see happen long term? What's the most far-fetched thing that will make you take a new approach to faith, focus, and love to obtain? Getting rid of your old ways, your old attitude, your old excuses, your old way of thinking.

That can seem like a sacrifice because you really have to take time to learn how to be the true, most unapologetic, and authentic you as possible. And a lot of times we put on characteristics and personality traits based on our environment or what we've been told that we should be by society. Sometimes changing your thought process, changing your desires, changing the way you look at the life around you can first seem like a sacrifice.

Deciding to do a fast, deciding to eat better, deciding to learn your blood type and eat for your blood type could be a sacrifice because some blood types need meat, and some need more vegetables, but the overall goal is balance in it all. If you are gung-ho on trying to follow the latest crowd, crave, or rave, then you may feel like you are sacrificing doing what's best for you. It might seem crazy to say, "I'm sacrificing the old me to do what's best for the new me," but that's letting go of the things that didn't work to grab hold of the things and promises that will work.

So anything given up for God's plan will be restored. This whole section is about sacrificing and the things that you may have to adjust and give up in order to reach the desired outcome or goal that you have planned, set, that you're praying for, or trying to intentionally manifest. Everything that you are willing to lose to obtain the best version of you will be replaced by what's meant for you because if you can lose it, then it wasn't meant. What is meant will come back a hundredfold.

What I've learned is sometimes we pray and desire things that aren't meant for us on our path and we can force those things to come to pass, but it will delay or distract something else that we may have been supposed to accomplish. You have to understand that restoration comes when you make yourself whole again.

When you go through all the things to manifest your faith, then you can manifest the results and those things that seem like they went away will be restored. It's a matter of thinking, what isn't a blessing is a lesson that will eventually turn back into a blessing. So it may seem like, oh man, something happened and it wasn't a blessing. You may feel like "It just, ruined me." And then you realize the lesson within it. You see the things that you could do differently, the changes that you can make, the decisions that you could have considered before so that you don't have to be sideswiped by something again.

The lesson will make sure things don't come out of nowhere in the future. So once you understand anything that is not a blessing is a potential lesson in which you are supposed to learn how to progress in, then once you learn how to progress through whatever that lesson is, it will indeed turn into a blessing.

A life of purpose really eliminates sacrifice. If you're living purposefully, if you are aligned with God, then there are some things that you're just not going to be into anymore. For some, disinterest will be the freedom in which sacrifices become blessings in disguise as you begin to think, "Okay, well, I didn't like this anyways, I wasn't really into that anyways. And now that I'm aligning with my purpose, with my oneness to the creator, now I can fully flourish in who I've been drawn to be within my soul, my entire life."

Journal Thoughts

So what do you do naturally? How does that come to the surface?

Are you burying who you are, in order to fit in? The question that I have for you now is what type of sacrifices can you make?

What type of sacrifices can you look back over your life and say, you know what?

That was a sacrifice that turned into a blessing because it was a lesson and I made the proper adjustments in order to get the ending result to be restored.

If there is anything else that you don't like the outcome of or with, what are you willing to do to become better? How can you grow by letting things go? What can you say that you know about yourself now that you've had your experiences and time to reflect?

Section 6: Being Set Aside

Now, for some people, this may come off as a form of isolation. However, it depends on your mindset about self-love and spending time alone and having me time.

It depends on your views of isolation and what you consider "me" time, getting to know yourself, and how you go about that. So overall, I want to first let you know that having time alone is very healthy. If you are always with a bunch of people or always with more than your spouse and your immediate family, and you can never spend time alone to yourself with your own thoughts, that's as unhealthy as always being isolated from everyone and never ever spending time with anyone outside of yourself.

Now, healthy isolation is taking time to get to know yourself, spending some time alone, and being one with your own thoughts. Taking time to meditate is a form of isolation because although you can meditate in a room full of other people, it is also good to learn how to meditate on your own by yourself. It's good to learn how to be alone so you can sit alone and speak with God, the creator, and the universe by yourself on your own.

So what's healthy isolation? Healthy isolation is having time alone where it does not make you sad, depressed, or lonely. Contrary to widely held belief, every person that spends a lot of time alone isn't lonely and every lonely person isn't alone. Some people feel alone in a room full of people, then some people feel completely alone in a room of nobody but themselves, but they feel full. They're full, not of themselves, but within themselves, they have peace.

So healthy isolation can come in phases. It can come in fasting. Fasting is staying away from something or restraining yourself from normal activity for a restricted amount of time or a certain amount of time.

So if you fast from social media, that is healthy isolation. If you spend a lot of time working with large groups of people and you take a week for yourself or you and your immediate family, your best friend, girlfriend, boyfriend, spouse, significant other, or with your children, that week break is healthy isolation.

When I say isolation can come in phases, you may not always want to be alone. You may not always want to feel alone, even if you're not lonely. So you may not be a person that is always with others or always alone. You may be able to find a balance where you spend time with others, but you also make time for yourself.

You can also do a spiritual detox and which is when you begin to detox yourself, your life, your mind from unhealthy things that could be negative talk within yourself, negative behavior that comes when others are around or by yourself. If you are having thoughts of harming yourself or harming others or if you are making plans to do such a thing, then you may need to get some company and talk to someone. However, if you are having those types of thoughts, then you need to begin to spiritually detox and begin to listen to healthy things, positive uplifting things to help your soul feel better.

Honestly, a spiritual detox can also mean fasting from church or spiritual practices so that God can speak to you on your own. However, church or any other religious service can also serve as a spiritual detox if you don't normally go. Your spiritual detox is going to be based on you.

For your spiritual detox, you may need to eliminate all the negative people in your life. May be your healthy isolation is figuring out who in your life is toxic and then having the courage to say, "I need to make distance for myself, I need to first voice how I feel," say what the problem or concern is. Once that is said and understood, if that continues, then you can begin to separate yourself.

As you begin to grow, as you begin to understand your purpose, as you begin to understand yourself better, you will come to realize that there are a lot of things, activities, material possessions, and people that do not fit into your lifestyle that you're building. They do not fit into your purpose, can't contribute to your purpose, and will only diminish or take away from the overall thing that you're working on.

In those instances, that is something that you have to detox from, a people detox. You'll have your phases of healthy isolation, spiritual detox, and the detox that you must do from people, which explained is just ridding yourself of people that do not bring positive energy, positive information, or good ideals.

So you may know people that gossip. For your people detox, in order to reach your highest levels, then you might need to get away from the people who gossip. Unless you're running a gossip column or a magazine that specializes in those things, then your goal should be to stay away from gossip.

If you know that you have a struggle dealing with any type of thing, if you're trying to quit drinking, but you hang around people that drink, then you need to people detox. The things that you want to change about yourself, the things that you would like to grow, the things that you would even like to know, you have to feed everything to your soul. Then you have to starve things you want to get rid of.

So when I say starve other things, let's say you have a pornography habit, an unhealthy addiction to porn, then you may need to detox from that so that you can gain and maintain self-control around sex and how often you watch it. I don't believe that watching porn is bad. I believe that having an "unhealthy addiction" to porn is bad.

So you need to incorporate some things into your life that take away the control that pornography may have over you. The goal of healthy isolation and being set aside is to recognize yourself, see yourself, accept yourself, and recognize the plans, purposes, and path of God. Then to kind of critique your life, align your life with the things, people, places, and thought processes that will take you down the right path to get to your purpose, and to have fulfillment within your life.

A part of healthy isolation and being set aside is meditation. That is where you take the time to be one with the universe, to be one with God, to know yourself more, to hear and listen to what your soul is trying to tell you.

Remember, unhealthy isolation is real. That's when you are just so alone that you feel lonely and you seek unhealthy ways to be connected to people, or you begin to feel like no one cares about you in the world. That comes from most times either neglect or unhealthy isolation.

So being alone with your thoughts and God is being set aside. I mean, no sounds. Have you ever been able to ride in a car with your thoughts with no sound? What type of thoughts do you have? Are you curating thoughts of positive energy and vibes of growth? A lot has to do with being set aside, like what information you're taking in.

Are you investing in your knowledge, into your understanding, into your wisdom? What type of books are you investing in yourself that can tell you about things that you're interested in spiritually, physically, health wise, and mentally? Find anything that you have an interest in, that you can learn about, that will help you become a better you. Those are the things that you need to do & invest in when you're set aside.

Being set aside is being pruned to be made ready for whatever is coming next. Some people are never set aside. Some people's lives and the things that their purposed to do may not take being set aside.

Everyone's purpose is different, but the deeper the spiritual aspect of your purpose and the deeper the mental aspect of your purpose, the more set aside you will be. The more set aside you are, the more power that you will see within and the more powerful you will become without your ego. Being set aside takes humility because when you're set aside, you may not have the opportunity to boast. You might not have the opportunity to brag, to go and be out and be around people to show everybody what's going on because you're set aside. You are sharpening who you are, learning more about yourself, and becoming one with your own thoughts. Time alone really sharpens your focus because if you're not feeding into things that you don't want for your future, then you'll feed into your own success.

So you may not be able to go to the club. It may go back to what we learned about sacrifice. But when you're purposeful, you will understand that that sacrifice (or what seems like a sacrifice to others) or something bad, is you growing into something new and manifesting your dreams.

Being set aside is about having time alone or with people that you're closely connected with. This is when God can prune you and help you become the best version of yourself. Being set aside is not always completely isolated. You may have other people around you that's able to support, help, influence, and encourage you.

So don't think that being set aside means that you have to be alone or that you will be lonely. Being set aside is being filled with purpose, surrounded by the things, the people, and the places that will help you to grow into your best, most whole version of yourself.

Time alone doesn't mean being lonely. It's about learning how to enjoy your own company. While being set aside, you may take yourself on movie dates. You may take yourself out to eat. Of course, this is not me saying, yes, you may.

This is me making suggestions of things that you can do on your own that will help you spend more time with yourself, and help you love on and understand yourself better. This also allows you the comfort of being one with yourself, accepting yourself, embracing yourself without the thoughts of others, without the suggestions of others, and building your confidence in what you know about yourself. It's important to build your confidence in how you feel and think. Learn your specific why, to all of the things that you see, want, or feel inside. Are you capable of taking some time and spoiling yourself? I know that if you have children, you may not be able to get too much time set aside. Like if a single person gets set aside, because they don't have children, they can take some time to be alone.

However, when you're a parent, there are no days off. There is rarely alone time. So you will have to structure it in ways for you to be able to meditate, to have time to take it all in, to actualize your life.

You have to make time to take yourself out on dates, to get dressed up just for you. You may need to take a pole dancing class that will help you gain confidence as a mother who can still be sexy. If you're a father, you may need to go take a boxing class so that you feel strong in yourself as a father.

We have to begin to feed our soul what our soul needs more of, but only you know what your soul needs more of. Do you have time to assess yourself, to enjoy yourself, not to always critique yourself, but to do an evaluation? Are you happy? If you are happy or when you are happy, what things contribute to your happiness? If you're not happy, what things are taking away from your happiness? Honestly, you should do this within your life periodically. In relationships, you both can fine-tune your relationship so that you continue to grow and continue to be better.

As you're setting your intentions, whatever you set your intentions for, this is your time to see it and say, "Okay, now I've set my intentions, I've done all of these other things, where am I at on the scale to reaching my goals? How do I remain focused to figure out what is the next step without the clutter of people's opinions, without the clutter of what people think that I should do or shouldn't do? How far I should be, or how far I think that I am." When you are set aside, you have time to do selfevaluations as well as evaluations on your business, personal, professional, spiritual, and physical life. Generally speaking, your whole health should be addressed during this set-aside time.

That means getting the opportunity to fine-tune your mind, listen to books, grow a little bit, and figure out where you are mentally, where you desire to be maturity level-wise, and where you are spiritually.

Here are some things to consider:

Spiritual Evaluation: Do you feel as connected to God as you desire to feel? What can you do to improve your relationship with God or to connect more deeply spiritually within yourself?

Financial Evaluation: where are you & where would you like to be? What things do you need to do in order to reach the goals that you have set for yourself financially? What may you have to cut back on? What may you have to give more into?

Mental Evaluation: where are you mentally? Where's your head space? How are you feeling? If you need to talk out loud to yourself so that you can tell yourself how you really feel versus just saying, "I'm okay" because you don't have time to address the issues that are at play. I want you to know it's okay to seek counseling. Seeing a therapist or a life coach might be the key to finding peace.

Remember, you need to be physically healthy as well. To fulfill the purpose that God has for you, you have to be willing to take care of yourself. You have to get a physical and get checkups.

If you have unaddressed health issues, address them so that you can get those things behind you and you can continue to focus on your purpose and goals. As you begin to get everything aligned, those things will push you into the divine time that will take you into your destiny. This may be a touchy topic because not everybody can practice what I'm about to say.

But if you are single, as in you have not met the man that you desire to marry and you are not in a governmentacknowledged marriage, or you are not in a live-in type of relationship. In some of these instances, you may feel single and may want to exit the relationship that you are in. That is not something that I can tell you that you need to do.

That is something that you have to evaluate and decide on your own.

Relationship Evaluation: Are you happy? Are you spiritually and mentally supported? Do you feel loved? Are you being abused, neglected, or anything that diminishes your mind, soul, body, or your finances? Because sometimes people can be in a financially abusive relationship as well. So if you are in a relationship and it is unhealthy, the first thing I would say is to seek counseling, so you can have a conversation.

If you are in a physically abusive relationship, I would say seek counseling and figure out steps and a plan in which you can save yourself from that abusive relationship.

Now for everybody else, if you are single and you are frolicking around sexually, that can become draining because you're picking up that energy from that person. Even when you're not talking about things, even when it's just sex or friends with benefits and there are no feelings attached, you still pick up that person's energy that they put inside of you or on you when you engage in sex.

Honestly, sex is a natural desire. Affection & physical touch are "Love Languages" which can cause you to love sex. Take a second to understand how much celibacy, even if only for a time, can help you with intimacy if you're single.

If you're married, don't go to your husband, talking about, uh, Speaking Freedom said we need to be celibate.

No, you do not withhold sex from your husband if you are married. I don't care if you're fighting. Unless you all have committed to a fast or some other form of agreement to restrain from sex, for a certain amount of time or a specific purpose. Maybe, you know, he's in the sports and it throws his game off.

Again, If you're married, don't go to your spouse saying you going to be celibate, you know, I'm not telling you to do that. We do not support that.

If you are married, have a significant other, and are in a fully committed relationship: have sex regularly, watch porn, have more sex, enjoy your relationship as much as possible and know that sex is important, I don't care if anybody tells you differently. Now, back to my single folks.

If you are single, consider celibacy not as a "do-all, fix-all religious type of thing," but consider celibacy for yourself. Consider the growth of self-control, the growth of development without having to deal with somebody else in that way. The reason why I suggest celibacy is because you want to hone in all of the positive energy that you have.

You don't want to give that away to random people and there is a great importance of the flow of energy, especially during sexual intercourse, but you also are able to master self-control. So celibacy does not have to be five years or two years. You can be celibate for six months if that's going to help you gain self-control, but be committed to whatever it is that you're deciding to do in order to maintain your being set aside. This allows God to speak to you clearly so that the creator of the universe can dwell within your being and you can honor your temple more.

Just a reminder, this is not about religion or waiting to get married. If you're engaged to your significant other, I definitely believe that sex can help you along but your marriage should not be based on sex. Now I'm going to stop talking about this because there's a whole other book for you about marriage, sex, love, and romance. With considering celibacy, think about self-control.

It's a part of being set aside. You may not want to be celibate. You will see the benefits of practicing celibacy if you try it.

However, if you don't want to be celibate, consider other ways to help yourself gain more self-control. That means if you are somebody who has a regular habit of doing anything that you enjoy, you may want to stop for six months, stop for a year, and not as a punishment but as a goal to gaining self-control. The worst thing that you could do is be someone with no self-control.

Self-control is not all about indulging in foods or indulging in sex or indulging in things like that. Self-control can be controlling your emotions so that you make a decision based on what you want and not based on the emotion that you feel at that given time. Self-control can help you not do things that other people just freely do.

Self-control can help you focus on building your empire, your brand, and your millionaire status in such a way that others cannot because they lack self-control. Self-control is a key component to your growth, to who you are as a person, and to your purpose. It's good to be spontaneous but you can be spontaneous with self-control.

Don't just do something just because you can do it. Selfcontrol evaluates to see how things play into your purpose, how it plays into your life, and how those things that you decide to do will affect others. The more selfcontrol you have, the higher that you will be able to go because when things come to tempt you, you won't be willing to just say yes, you will be able to say no to things that are not good for your soul.

Journal Thoughts

How can you move in a set-aside way?

Sometimes being set aside is saying "I may hang out but I don't hang out as much. I may indulge in something that I like but I don't do it all the time. I may want to hang out with my friends, but I don't hang out with my friends all day every day where I don't get anything accomplished that's productive."

Being set aside is about having focus. Having self-control is about being able to maintain that focus. So what can you do to be more set aside, to be more focused, to be more driven towards your destiny while focusing on your purpose?

Section 7: No Mistakes

This is probably one of the most controversial sections in this particular book because people think that you can make mistakes while living and experiencing life for the first time. When I say there are no mistakes, if you decide to continue down a path that is not for you, that is not necessarily a mistake because you're making a conscious decision to continue down that path. However, if while on that path, you learn something new, decide to do something new, then decide to go down a different path; you just decided to go down a different path.

There are no mistakes if you can learn from what you didn't like or what you didn't know. So that means that if you go through a life experience and don't like the results, causing you to change paths. Find the learning moment and use that for the learning curve.

It's an opportunity for you to have a lesson. It's a learning challenge. When I say it's a learning challenge, consider that if you've never done something before, never got that experience before or you're seeking a different result, along the way you have to try different things until you learn what works. Then based on the results, the experience and how you are able to take from that will teach you how to adjust moving forward.

Every learning experience won't be enjoyable, but every learning experience should teach you something new. Just look back over things that you've experienced if you didn't like the result or the experience go back and grow from it. You should be thinking, what can I learn about myself, the situation, and where I would like to go from whatever I've experienced and the results that came from that? So if you go to school and you don't enjoy the subject matter in which you are learning, you may change classes if you're in college.

But if that subject matter is not enjoyed because it's difficult, but it's teaching you, then you may endure that and endure not liking the class because you're learning. Every lesson will not be enjoyable because sometimes you have to grow through tough things to learn about yourself, your thinking, how you process information, and the beliefs that you take from different situations. But there is absolutely no mistake if you are learning something along the way.

Let's say you make a bad decision, not a bad decision based on what other people think, but a decision that later in life You simply don't like. Whatever the experience was that you did not care for, if you take the time to review that experience and the result, then as you process through that experience, you should be able to pinpoint where that particular experience may have veered to one result versus another. You will be able to see where you could have done something differently, gotten a different result at the end, or had a different experience based on the way you comprehend. The goal is not to dismiss all bad experiences.

The goal is to learn from anything that you do not like, just as much as you learn from the things that you do like. Everything in life is teaching you something. Every experience, every conversation, every situation that you experience in every way possible, everything that you go through in life should be teaching you something.

You can ignore the lesson. However, it may block your blessing down the line. Imagine, if you face the same thing over again, but you didn't take the lesson from the first time, then you'll end up in that situation again with the same result unless you make the adjustments in your life that reflect the end result or the experience that you would prefer to have versus the one that you're facing. What does it take to really get the results that you desire? What are the goals that you set from your intentions at the beginning?

You were told to write down some things, to think about some things, and to meditate on those intentions throughout the course of this book. What does it take to get you that desired result? If you are an entrepreneur or a person who seeks to do things on your own, you may be in the midst of already doing something. This applies to every area of your life.

If you're cooking the same dish three times and the first time you like one part of it, but you don't like something else; then the second time, the goal is to make the adjustments, and make changes to learn how to do it better. Think to yourself, I did this, I like this step and this ingredient was good. Okay, if I take away this ingredient, it may make it better, than making that adjustment, so by the third time you have it perfect. It is the same way for everything that you do in life, for every experience, for every situation, for every result, for every thought.

You have to evaluate by saying, "Okay, if I was thinking like this, then how can I change my thinking so that I can think better so that I can do better, and so that I can be better?" If you're in an abusive relationship, your goals have to be to figure out how do I stop the abuse. Abuse can be stopped in two different ways. This can be stopped with treatment or by leaving.

Sometimes you can be in a mildly abusive relationship, get treatment together jointly, and grow in such a way that where the abuse stops without you having to leave. But for abuse to stop, you have to get the proper treatment so that you can address the issues. Saying "No mistakes" is not about right or wrong, it's how it helps you become a better person. How did it help you and equip you for the things that you want to get into? So what results do you desire? How does reflecting on the different stages of your life, the different stages of who you are as a person, help you grow into the desired results that you have set for yourself? What can be done differently in everything that you do so that you don't get the same results? Normally, what I suggest is, that if you made one decision, you didn't like the result and you were in the same exact situation, try choosing the other thing.

In Spiritual Human Behavior, there is a theory that addresses this particular topic about how to make better decisions and how to make adjustments so that you can get the results that you desire. Today, we are focusing on that there are no mistakes in the course of learning and growing through life. Your mistakes are normally based on somebody else's experiences and what they believe should be right or wrong.

But for you, you have to come up with your own experiences. You have to make your own life choices. Your life choices will determine where you go long-term. But what can be done differently? So let's take generational curses or habitual family problems.

If in your family, you recognize a pattern, how do you break the cycle of that bad thing or generational curse so that you change the pattern within your family? So if in your family, people are normally neglected and abused, they accept anything or don't fully go for their dreams, it is your job as a person who desires to grow to figure out how you take your family on a different route, a different role, on a different path so that you can get a different result than the people that came before you. What results did your ancestors gain?

How could you help or develop or change those results so that you can grow more and take your family legacy a step further? What did the experience tell you about you? A lot of times we look at different things that we've gone through and we look to blame other people for things that we need to be accountable for. So what are you learning about yourself from your bad experiences, the things that you don't like, the results that you get for something that you went through? What are you learning about you? How is that shaping your goals? What are your experiences telling you about your thought process in life? How you think will tell you what type of experiences you have in your life. How you program your mind, how you set your thought process, the information that you take in, what you feed into, the faith that you have, and the intentions that you have set will tell you a lot about where you are going. It will tell you what type of goals you will reach and the things that are truly important to you. When you're talking about generational things or correcting problems that you see as a pattern, you have to address yourself. After being set aside, there are a lot of things that you're going to address within yourself, about yourself and you really have to begin to change the patterns of unfruitful things.

You have to change the bad patterns that you do not like, whether it's your behavior, your thinking, your spending, your spiritual practices, or the habits that maintain your health. But you need to accept your past. Every bad experience helped you grow.

Every bad experience was designed to teach you something that you needed to know.

This section of this book should help you reflect on the things that helped you become who you are today and accept the experience. Unfortunately, bad things happen and in those instances, we have to figure out what can we learn about how it changed us, how that made us grow, how it made us change the way we move forward and make peace with the things that you have encountered or experienced and make those adjustments as well.

So that if you got a result that you didn't like before, you've addressed the issue within and then you've made the adjustments to help you ensure that those bad experiences don't happen again. You also have to accept your present because where you are is a portion of where you've been and what you're feeding yourself now. Your present needs to be accepted and embraced.

You have to make peace with where you are at right now today, where your mind is, where your thinking is, where your heart is. What do you desire right now? Accept where you are right now so that you can plan to grow for your future and where you desire to be. As you begin to make and create goals, dreams, and vision boards, you have to accept where you're saying you want your future to be.

If you don't accept where you want your future to be, then it will be hard to make plans to get to the goals that you're saying that you want to see. If you set goals without making any adjustments, then you might not reach your goals, it might make you depressed and it might make you feel some type of way. When you're not doing the things that you feel in your heart, it begins to weigh on you. Making adjustments so that you can advance towards the goal, the vision, and what you see for your future is most important.

Evaluate where you are right now. What can you do?
What adjustments do you need to make for your future? What can you understand about your core, from everything that you've experienced, past & present? You must understand how those things play into who you will be in the future, how you will

grow in the future, and what you will grow into doing.

It's important to evaluate how has life changed you. What have those good experiences done to help you grow? What have they encouraged? What have they discouraged? What are those bad experiences? And how did they change your perception of the world around you? A lot of people blame themselves or blame others for certain instances and it keeps you bound to it because you're not accepting that it happened. Acceptance comes with disgruntlement because you're not seeing the lesson in that experience and how it shaped you to your core. When you begin to understand what your core is and how things shaped you, then you will be able to make a plan for your future.

Because the things that make you, you, the things that you experience help shape you for your purpose. But in order for those things to do that, you have to stop thinking that everything was a mistake. You have to stop thinking that somebody else has a perfect life.

You have to be willing to realize that life is a journey that everybody has to face. Everybody is learning, so there are really no mistakes. Understand, that because everybody's learning, we can all learn from each other. Not only is everybody learning, but knowing that everybody's meant to experience a different life hopefully gives you peace of mind.

So after you've accepted all of your past and all of your present, and you accept where you desire to go in your future, then you have to forgive yourself. Accept and forgive yourself for either getting yourself in regretful situations or not recognizing where you could have been better. Accept the times when you believe that you've heard God speaking to you, guiding you, and you didn't listen.

Accept every bad thing and then forgive yourself for not knowing more because you're learning. I want you to get that part in your mind. You are learning based on your course and your path through this journey of life.

Now, once you begin to forgive yourself, you will be able to forgive others. The key to forgiveness is realizing that we all do some messed up things sometimes. We all experience some things that make us do things that may cause another person to have a bad experience, but not forgiving ourselves or not forgiving others will not help us progress.

It will leave us with an icky feeling on the inside and that icky feeling becomes dis-ease, which is disease. So the goal is to begin to forgive people and accept people. You don't have to deal with a person that you've forgiven, but accept that they may have honestly done something that may not have been pleasant, may not have been good, or whatever the case may be.

But knowing that you've needed forgiveness, knowing that you've done things, you should be able to extend that forgiveness and allow that person grace. Grace does not mean that you are allowing that person back into your life. You may forgive that person and dismiss that person.

It may be healthy for you to keep certain people out of your lives after you've forgiven them. But I don't want you to walk around with that unforgiveness in your heart towards another person because then you will begin to harvest unforgiveness for yourself. If you're judging people for mistakes or the course of life that they've had to endure in the way they've learned to survive, then you will also judge yourself more harshly.

Most times, the people who judge others harshly have already begun to judge themselves or they feel judged because they're around people who judge, gossip, and contribute to that energy of unsettlement. Moving forward with confidence is easy once you begin to accept yourself. Once you begin to embrace all of who you are, past, and present, and what you desire to do in the future, moving forward is easier when you're not holding things against people that are no longer in your life. If you dismiss them from your life, then forgive them so that they're not renting space in your mind while they're off living their life. If you forgive people, then you can let them go and you don't have to have any negative feelings towards anyone at all. So when you move forward with confidence, you're just moving forward with less baggage. You're moving forward with a free mentality towards whatever the things that you desire to be because you're not holding anything against anyone else.

You're not holding anything against yourself because you believe in your own freedom. You allow other people to experience that freedom at whatever distance or closeness that God allowed them to have in your life.

How can these things help you reach your goals? Well, just generally speaking, when you begin to speak about not making mistakes, you become less critical of the things that you're doing right based on the things that you did wrong, based on people's opinions.

When you become less critical of what you did wrong or right and you begin to evaluate based on progression and focus, then you will be able to excel more, do more, experience more, and be more. Learn and understand that people make decisions based on things that are going on within themselves. A lot of things that you experience that is bad come from another person, it has nothing to do with who you are, or something that you've done.

You have to learn not to take things personally that don't reflect you. How someone makes you feel is more a reflection of them. How you make other people feel is more of a reflection on you.

Journal Thoughts

Where do you see yourself going if there was nothing that you could do wrong, if there were no mistakes that could be made and you just went towards and started following your purpose?

How could you reach your goals based on realizing that you're not making mistakes?

You're simply learning and gaining your confidence in who you are, your gifts, your abilities, your purpose, and where you desire to be. I would like to ask you, how has this information impacted what you set for your intentions?

In the next book, Faith 201, we will ask you to set different intentions. So this book was solely based on the intentions that were set.

Final Question: How can you reflect, learn, and grow from the information within this book to help you manifest the intentions of your heart?

Thank you for your purchase. Please check out our other books.

Spiritual Human Behavior
Faith 201
Faith 301
Faith 401
The Unknown Power of A New Believer
It's My Time

www.ingramcontent.com/pod-product-compliance
Lightning Source LLC
Chambersburg PA
CBHW070155080526
44586CB00015B/2001